HOCUS-POCUS MAGICAL COOKBOOK

Written by
Donna Boundy

Illustrated by
Julia Gran

innovative KIDS™

CONTENTS

WAYS OF THE WIZARD (Introduction) 4

Wizard Purposes

To Spread Silliness 6

To Bring About Adventure 8

To Create Family Harmony . . . 10

To Be Smarter in School 12

To Bring On a Sunny Mood. . . 14

To Have a Good Hair Day 15

To Make the Day Go
Smoothly 15

To Create the Urge to Dance . . 16

To Bring About Good Health . . 18

To Be Less Grumpy. 20

To Be as Cool as Can Be 22

To Keep Friends Forever 24

To Make Imaginations
Run Wild. 26

To Energize for Sports 28

To Make Dreams Come True . . 30

To Make a Surprise Arise 32

To See into the Future 34

To Be the Best You Can Be . . . 36

To Bubble Trouble Away 37

To Be an Amazing Cook 38

To Build Strong Muscles 40

To Sharpen Math Skills 41

To Ace Your Homework 42

To Share and Share Alike . . . 44

To Calm Your Worries 46

To Dare to Try
Something New 48

To Keep the Doctor Away 50

To Bring Love into Your Life . . 52

To Hang Out and Party 54

To Make Something Creative . . 56

To Clean Up in a Flash 58

To See Things in a New Way. . 60

To Make People Laugh 62

To Keep Scary Things Away . . 64

To Bring On Beautiful
Weather 66

To Make You Jump for Joy . . . 68

To Bring On a Good Night's
Sleep 70

To Bring On Magical Dreams . 71

To Make World Peace 72

WACKY WIZARD BREAKFASTS 6

Hocus-Pocus Pancakes 6
Enchanted Eggs 8
Full Moon French Toast 10
Vanishing Yogurt Sundae 12
Positive Potions 14

LIGHTNING LUNCHES 16

Mysterious Macaroni
  & Charming Cheese 16
Chicken Noodle Doodle Soup 18
Totally Tempting Tomato Soup . . 20
Kettle o' Cukes Soup 22
Dipped Cheese Sandwich 24
Kitchen Sink Salad 26
Pa'sketti Marinara 28
Palm Reader's Pita Pockets 30
Taco Treasures 32
Soothsayer's Spuds 34
Glittering Rice and Bubbling
  Sweet Beans 36
New Moon Noodles 38
Sorcerer's Spinach and
  Conjurer's Corn 40

TRICKSTER TIDBITS 42

Know-It-All Nachos 42
Pizza Pizzazz 44
Wizard Wraps 46
Dungeon Dips 48
Abracadabra Applesauce 50
Plenty of Love Potions 52

DISAPPEARING DESSERTS AND DRINKS 54

Faerie Fruit Kabobs 54
Mango-Tango Pudding 56
Bibbity-Bobbity Brownies 58
Cosmic Cookies 60
Snicker-Doodles 62
Smooshy S'mores 64
Apple Cauldron Cobbler 66
Jump-for-Joy Jelly Rolls 68
Bedtime Brews 70
Peace Potion 72

Ways of the Wizard

Be sure to read these pages first!

Positive Potions

Following a recipe is a lot like making magic. You add this and stir that, heat this up and cool that down, and you have just created something special!

Potions are usually cooked up with a purpose (to make someone fall in love or to see into the future). In this book, every recipe has a positive "wizard purpose"—to clean up in a flash, to make people laugh, even to calm your worries. Do these purposes really work? That just might be up to you!

Wizard-Speak

This cookbook contains some very special wizard words. **Elementals** are the *ingredients* you will need for a recipe. When a recipe calls for using a **beaker**, use *a 1-cup measuring cup*. And if the instructions say to put ingredients into a **cauldron**, put them in a *pot on the stove* for heating.

Every recipe calls for one **special magic ingredient**. Say it out loud or unscramble it to try to figure out the common name for that food. If you're still

not sure, look it up on the Wizard Wheel on the inside front cover. Then say the **magic rhyme or chant** aloud while waving your magic wand, and you'll put the purpose into the potion!

Cool Experiments — and More

In addition to great recipes, each page presents interesting facts and fun experiments you can do. How do you make Oookey-Ooze? Are cucumbers really "cool"? Did you know there's a museum just for noodles? This cookbook will answer these questions and more.

Wizard Wheel

Inside the front cover is a wheel that will help you *convert*, or exchange, amounts or ingredients. The outer ring will give you the common name for special magic ingredients. The inner rings will give you equivalents and will help you convert the U.S. system of measurements into the *metric* system. Just turn the rings, match the dots, and read what equals what!

4

WISE WIZARD SAFETY TIPS
Read and follow these rules!

 You'll see this symbol in the "Elementals" pot wherever a **recipe will require a grown-up**.

MAGIC WAND: Do not put the wand that comes with this book in the food, in boiling water, in hot oil, or in a microwave oven.

WASH UP: Whenever you cook, begin by washing your hands. Wash them again and clean surfaces after handling raw chicken or meat or raw egg mixtures.

POT HANDLES: Always turn pot handles away from the edge of the stove, so that you don't accidentally knock the pot off and burn yourself.

KITCHEN KNIVES AND PEELERS: Knives and peelers can be very sharp, so pay close attention to what you are doing. Cut or peel away from your body.

MICROWAVE OVENS: Never put foil or anything made of metal in a microwave oven, as these can cause damage. Microwaved food can be very hot, so be careful.

OVEN MITTS: Wear oven mitts when stirring or handling hot pots, pans, or microwaved food, and when pouring or stirring hot water.

STIRRING THE POT: It's best to stir pots with a long-handled wooden spoon. Metal utensils can get hot and burn your fingers.

HEATING OIL: Never walk away and leave a skillet with oil on the stove. Oil can catch on fire easily.

DRAINING PASTA: The boiling water and steam from cooking noodles can burn, so be careful when draining them. Hold the pan with oven mitts and then pour the water slowly into the drainer so it doesn't splash.

MIXERS AND BLENDERS: Always unplug a mixer before putting beaters in or taking them out. And be sure to turn the blender off before putting a spoon in or scraping the sides.

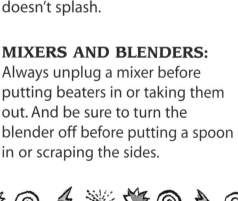

To Spread Silliness

Hocus-Pocus Pancakes

3/4 beaker flour
1/2 teaspoon salt
1 teaspoon *puffupalredia*
1 egg
1 tablespoon melted butter (or vegetable oil)
1/4 beaker milk

1. Put flour and salt into a bowl.
2. Add **puffupalredia**.
   Stir wand above bowl in spirals, and say these magic words, as quickly as you can:

> Silli-silli-bo-billi
> Banana-fana-fo-filli
> Fee-fi-mo-milli—**Silly!**

3. In another bowl, beat egg.
4. Add beaten egg, butter (or oil), and milk to flour concoction.
5. Stir until everything is moist. There will still be lumps—that's OK.
6. Put skillet on stove top at medium-high heat. It's ready when drops of cold water sprinkled on it bounce and dance around.
7. Pour about 1/4 beaker of batter into skillet for each pancake. Turn heat down to medium.

Elementals

8. Cook until tops of pancakes are covered with bubbles. Then ease a spatula under the edge of each pancake until it lifts all the way around.

9. Flip it over.

10. Cook until both sides are a nice medium-brown color. Remove immediately and serve with maple or strawberry syrup!

Makes 6 small pancakes or 3 giant ones

Strawberry Syrup

This is a great topping for pancakes!

1 beaker strawberries

2 tablespoons orange juice

1 beaker maple syrup

Mash up the strawberries and put them in a small cauldron with the orange juice. Add the syrup and simmer for 5 minutes over medium heat. Spoon over pancakes!

0 − 1 X 2 DOUBLE TROUBLE + 8 ÷ 9 X

If you want to cook for other wizards (or grown-ups), you will have to "double" this recipe. That means that you will have to multiply the amounts of all the ingredients by 2. Do the math! The whole numbers are easy. But the fractions are tricky. Here's how to multiply a fraction. We'll use 3/4 beaker flour as an example.

STEP 1: Setting Up

Write the 2 like a fraction: $\frac{2}{1}$ is the same as 2.

Put the fraction you want to multiply ($\frac{3}{4}$) next to it, so the problem looks like this:

$$\frac{3}{4} \times \frac{2}{1}$$

STEP 2: Multiplying

Multiply the top half:

$$3 \times 2 = 6$$

Then multiply the bottom half:

$$4 \times 1 = 4$$

ANSWER: $\frac{6}{4}$

STEP 3: Subtracting

$\frac{4}{4}$ is the same as 1. So $\frac{6}{4}$ is more than 1. How much more?

ANSWER: $\frac{2}{4}$ more

So $\frac{6}{4}$ is the same as saying 1 and $\frac{2}{4}$.

STEP 4: Reducing

If both the top and bottom of a fraction can be divided evenly by the same number (try 2), do that next. $\frac{2}{4} \div 2$ What do you get?

ANSWER: $\frac{1}{2}$ (1 and $\frac{2}{4}$ is the same as $1\frac{1}{2}$)

So $\frac{3}{4}$ beaker doubled is $1\frac{1}{2}$ beakers!

Now double the other elementals in the recipe, and you'll have enough for 2!

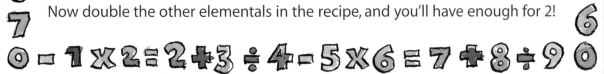

To Bring About Adventure

2 or 3 eggs

3 tablespoons *kumsfrumakow*

1 tablespoon butter

1 sprinkle salt (optional)

1/4 beaker shredded cheese (any kind)

Enchanted Eggs

1. Break eggs into a bowl and mix well with a fork.

2. Add **kumsfrumakow**.

   Say these magic words three times, while waving your wand over the concoction:

   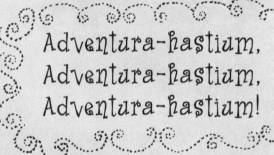

   Adventura-hastium,
   Adventura-hastium,
   Adventura-hastium!

3. Melt butter in frying pan over medium-high heat. When melted, sprinkle the butter with salt.

4. Pour egg concoction into pan. Have a spatula ready.

5. Using a wooden spoon, scrape eggs from edge toward center of pan, turning over and over as it cooks.

6. As the eggs are firming up, add the shredded cheese. Continue turning over in pan till the eggs are cooked.

Serves 1

Elementals

Thundering Toast Toppers

With or without Enchanted Eggs, toast doesn't have to be ordinary. To "spread" even more adventure in your day, try these easy toppers.

Cream Cheese or Peanut Butter and More

Instead of butter, spread cream cheese or peanut butter on toast. Top that with jelly, honey, raisins, apple slices, crushed pineapple, crumbled walnuts, or chopped dates. Yum!

Cinnamon Toast

Mix together 1 teaspoon of sugar with 1/4 teaspoon of cinnamon. Butter the toast the second it pops up. Sprinkle the cinnamon mixture over the toast.

Egg in a Hole

Use a small juice glass to cut a hole in a piece of light toast. Butter both sides and put toast in a frying pan on medium heat. Crack and drop 1 egg into the center and cook for 1 or 2 minutes. Turn it all over with a spatula and cook the same on other side.

Banana Toast

Butter the toast and cover it with thin slices of banana. Drizzle honey over the whole thing!

CENTER OF GRAVITY

Be an "eggs-pert" in telling a raw egg from a hard-boiled egg without cracking it open. How? Test its *center of gravity*!

Everything has a center of gravity. That's the point around which the weight of something is spread out or balanced.

TRY THIS EXPERIMENT

Lay an egg down on its side and spin it. Does it spin easily, or does it wobble? If it spins easily, it's hard-boiled; if it wobbles, it's raw!

The raw egg wobbles because the yolk and white are still in liquid form. They are sloshing around inside the eggshell when you spin it. The center of gravity keeps changing. A hard-boiled egg has turned to solid from the heat, so its center of gravity doesn't change. This lets it spin faster!

To Create Family Harmony

Full Moon French Toast

3 eggs
1/2 beaker milk
1 pinch **nomannic**
1 tablespoon butter
5 slices bread

Elementals

1. Whisk the eggs and milk together in a shallow bowl. (Whisk means to stir briskly with a fork or "whisker.")

2. Add **nomannic**.

   Hold the wand over the egg concoction and invite a family member to hold your other hand. Repeat these words:

   By the light of the moon
   Or the morning sun,
   I'll get along
   With everyone.

3. Heat a skillet on medium heat. Put half of the butter in it and let it melt.

4. Using a fork, dip one piece of bread into the egg mixture. Turn it over so that both sides get soaked. Dip a second piece.

5. Put the soaked bread into the heated skillet.

6. When the bottoms are golden brown, use a spatula to flip each piece to the other side.

7. When those two slices are done, remove to a plate and cook the others the same way. (Keep the first two warm in a toaster oven on low heat.)

Serves 2 (with one slice left over to share—harmoniously!)

Blueberry Syrup

1/2 beaker blueberries (fresh, or frozen and thawed)

2 tablespoons orange juice

1 beaker maple syrup

Mash the blueberries with the back of a fork. Put them in a small cauldron with orange juice and maple syrup. Simmer for 5 minutes over medium heat. Pour over hot French toast!

CHEW ON THIS

French toast isn't really French. But we use a lot of words that don't mean what they usually mean. Many of our *expressions* (colorful ways of saying things) refer to food. We say she brings home the *bacon*, but he's also got a lot of *bread*. Or maybe he's a *crab* because he doesn't have any *dough* right now. If you have a *beef* with someone, you could *chew* her out, or *grill* her about what happened, and then *butter* her up. If you're a real *ham*, you could get in a *jam* or a *pickle*, and then *stew* about it for a while. Someone stop me before I go *nuts*…I mean, this is no *picnic*! There are a lot of other food expressions. Can you name some more?

To Be Smarter in School

1 beaker yogurt
(plain or vanilla)

1 banana

2 tablespoons honey

1/4 beaker granola

1 teaspoon
leftowtaweet

Vanishing Yogurt Sundae

1. Spoon yogurt into a sundae dish or a shallow bowl.
2. Cut the banana in slices and place the pieces around the yogurt.
3. Drizzle honey and sprinkle granola over the top.
4. Sprinkle *leftowtaweet* on top.

   Hold wand over yogurt concoction and repeat this command:

Math or reading,
Spelling or art,
Science or history—
Help make me smart!

Serves 1

$E=MC^2$

Elementals

Other Smart Toppings

Get smart! Experiment with other great sundae toppers.
Choose one or mix and match!

Chopped apples	Raisins	Grapes (cut in half)
Cubes of melon	Sliced peaches	Chocolate chips
Diced pineapple	Sunflower seeds	Sliced almonds
Sesame seeds	Chopped walnuts	Your favorite cereal
Raspberries	Blueberries	Sliced strawberries
Pitted cherries		Maple syrup

ALWAYS ON SUNDAE

Ever wonder why we call concoctions with yogurt or ice cream and toppings "sundaes"?

It all started back in 1890 in Evanston, Illinois. Lots of people then liked ice cream sodas (milk with flavored syrup, soda fizz, and ice cream). But a town law made it *illegal* (against the law) to sell "stimulating beverages" (like fizzy sodas) on Sundays. Sunday was considered the holy day of rest.

One man who ran a "soda fountain" (a kind of ice cream parlor) started offering his customers big dishes of ice cream with syrup on Sunday—leaving out the soda fizz, so he wouldn't be breaking the law. He called his new concoction a "sundae"!

POSITIVE POTIONS

These potions will start you off on a magical day. No matter which one you choose, the steps are all the same—and easy!

1. Put all of the ingredients for the recipe you wish to make into a blender, adding the magical ingredient last.

2. Wave the magic wand as instructed.

3. Blend until smooth and pour into a glass to serve.

Each serves 1

To Bring On a Sunny Mood

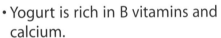

Swigs of Sunshine

1 beaker orange juice
1/2 beaker yogurt (plain or vanilla)
1 *ananab*

Wave your wand over the blender and sing out happily:

Shine on me, sun,
Whisk clouds away.
Make me feel bright
All through the day.

JUST SAY "YO"

Yogurt is so good tasting and has so many benefits, it's almost magic all by itself!

• Yogurt is rich in B vitamins and calcium.

• It contains good *bacteria*, which your intestines need to keep you healthy.

• It's a lot easier to digest than milk is.

• It soothes stomach ulcers.

• Some people even say it leads to long life!

To Have a Good Hair Day
Troll's Tonic

1 beaker milk

1 ripe peach, skinned, pitted, and cut in chunks
(or 1/2 beaker blueberries)

1/3 beaker low-fat cottage cheese

1 tablespoon honey

1 teaspoon vanilla extract

1 dash **megnut**

Wave the wand over your head and repeat:

Cowlicks and frizzies
Get out of sight.
My hair will look good
From morning till night.

To Make the Day Go Smoothly
Bahama Breakfast

1/4 beaker orange juice

1/2 beaker pineapple juice

1/2 banana

2 ice cubes

1 tablespoon
shredded, sweetened
coco-loco-nutty

If possible, put on some sunglasses and get real relaxed for this one. Wave your wand in easy circles toward the blender, softly saying:

Coco-loco-nutty,
Coco-loco-loo,
Make the day go easy,
Make the day go
SMOOOOTH!

To Create The Urge To Dance

1/2 tablespoon butter
(or nonstick oil spray)

1/2 box (8 ounces) dry macaroni
in your favorite shape

1 beaker shredded mild cheese
(such as cheddar, American,
or Monterey Jack)

1 1/4 beakers milk

1/2 beaker ricotta cheese

1/4 beaker grated Parmesan cheese

1/2 teaspoon salt

1/4 teaspoon pepper

1/4 beaker **krumblium**

Mysterious Macaroni & Charming Cheese

1. Preheat the oven to 350 degrees.
2. Butter the bottom of a casserole dish (or spray with nonstick oil).
3. Fill a large cauldron 2/3 full of water and place on high heat.
4. When the water boils, drop in the macaroni. (Watch out for splashes!)
5. Turn the heat to medium-high and boil macaroni for 8 to 10 minutes or follow time on box. Stir occasionally with a wooden spoon.
6. While macaroni is cooking, put shredded cheese into a bowl and add milk, cheeses, salt, and pepper. Pour mixture into casserole dish.

Elementals

7. When macaroni is done, drain the hot water off by pouring it all into a colander in the sink. Rinse briefly with cold water. (This keeps it from sticking together.) Shake colander to make sure you have all the water out!

8. Pour cooked, drained macaroni into casserole dish. Carefully blend macaroni with the cheese and milk mixture.

9. Sprinkle the special magic ingredient, **krumblium**, over the top.

Now you're ready for the magic words. Sway to the sound of your favorite dance music and wave your wand in figure eights over the mixture, saying:

Mumbo jumbo,
Charming cheese,
Twist and turn me
As you please!

10. Cover casserole with foil and bake for 30 minutes. (You may feel a strong urge to do the cha-cha while it's cooking, so you better set an oven timer!)

11. After 30 minutes, remove foil from dish (use oven mitts) and cook for 5 more minutes to lightly brown the top.

Serves 4

ANYONE FOR CURDS AND WHEY?

You've probably heard the old rhyme: "Little Miss Muffet, sat on a tuffet, eating her curds and whey...." But did you ever wonder what curds are? Or wish that your mom would cook up some whey? Well, when you eat your macaroni and cheese, you will actually be eating a little bit like Miss Muffet.

Before most dairy milk was *homogenized* (heated and treated to make the fat globs break into tiny particles), it would naturally separate into *curds* (the solid part that eventually can become cheese) and *whey* (the liquid that was drained off; it looks a bit like skimmed milk). Now we just call it cheese and milk!

To Bring About Good Health

3 chicken breasts,
with skin and bone

2 carrots

1 onion

1 celery stalk

1 teaspoon salt

1/4 teaspoon pepper

a few sprigs *curlyurby*

1 cup egg noodles
(the very thin ones,
or alphabet noodles)

Chicken Noodle Doodle Soup

1. Rinse chicken in cold water and place in a large cauldron.
2. Peel and slice carrots. Peel and chop onion. Wash and slice celery stalk.
3. Add vegetables to cauldron, along with salt and pepper.
4. Fill cauldron with enough cold water to cover everything, plus about 2 inches more.
5. Add *curlyurby.*
6. Shake your magic wand over the soup several times, as if sprinkling in "good health," and say:

Noodle-doodle-doo,
Noodle-doodle-dee,
Make me feel healthy
And strong as can be.

Elementals

7. Place cauldron on burner on high heat. Bring to a boil. Use a big spoon to skim off any foam that forms on top of the boiling mixture. (Wear oven mitts for this job!)

8. Reduce heat to low and simmer 1 to 2 hours, until the meat begins to fall off the bones.

9. Remove chicken from soup and let it cool until you can handle it (about 15 minutes). Turn off heat.

10. Boil the noodles in another cauldron with 3 beakers of water until they are tender. Drain.

11. Pull the cooled chicken meat and skin off the bone. Cut the meat in chunks and return only the meat to the soup.

12. Add cooked noodles and reheat soup for 1or 2 minutes more. Use a ladle to serve soup.

Makes 8 healthy servings

GOOD FOR WHAT AILS A WIZARD?

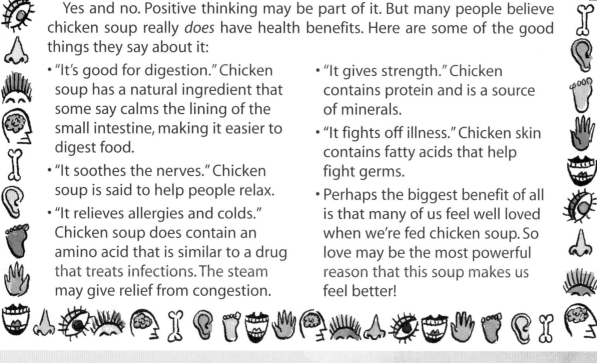

Chicken soup is a common "prescription" for colds, the flu, and feeling "under the weather." But does it really make you feel better?

Yes and no. Positive thinking may be part of it. But many people believe chicken soup really *does* have health benefits. Here are some of the good things they say about it:

- "It's good for digestion." Chicken soup has a natural ingredient that some say calms the lining of the small intestine, making it easier to digest food.

- "It soothes the nerves." Chicken soup is said to help people relax.

- "It relieves allergies and colds." Chicken soup does contain an amino acid that is similar to a drug that treats infections. The steam may give relief from congestion.

- "It gives strength." Chicken contains protein and is a source of minerals.

- "It fights off illness." Chicken skin contains fatty acids that help fight germs.

- Perhaps the biggest benefit of all is that many of us feel well loved when we're fed chicken soup. So love may be the most powerful reason that this soup makes us feel better!

To Be Less Grumpy

(works on others too!)

Totally ♪ Tempting ♪ Tomato Soup

1 onion

2 cloves garlic

3 tablespoons olive oil

1/2 teaspoon salt

a few sprigs fresh parsley

28-ounce can crushed tomatoes

1 beaker milk

1/2 beaker half-and-half

1/4 teaspoon *rymzwithfil*

Elementals

1. Chop the onion and set it aside.

2. Squeeze garlic cloves through a garlic press (or chop them finely if you don't have a press).

3. Put olive oil in bottom of medium-sized cauldron on the stove. Turn burner to medium.

4. Sauté (cook in oil) the onion and garlic for 5 to 10 minutes, stirring often to keep them from burning. When done, onions are soft and "see-through."

5. Add salt; chop parsley and add to onions.

6. Open can of tomatoes and put them and their liquid into a blender. Blend on high.

7. Pour the blended tomatoes into the cauldron with the onion mixture and heat until good and hot.

NO MORE TEARS!

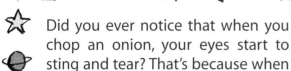

Did you ever notice that when you chop an onion, your eyes start to sting and tear? That's because when you cut into the onion, its juice *evaporates* quickly into the air—heading straight for your eyes! When something evaporates, it changes from liquid form to a gas. So the onion juice has become "onion gas."

But here's a wizard trick for cutting onions WITHOUT crying:

Place the onion in a bowl of cold water. Peel and slice or chop it while it's under the water. The vapors won't be able to evaporate and sting your eyes!

8. Add milk and **rymzwithfil**. Wave your wand over the soup potion, saying:

> Grumpus away-from-us!
> Grumpus away-from-us!
> Grumpus away-from-us!

9. Heat soup a few minutes more—but don't boil it. Serve with fresh bread or sandwiches.

Makes 4 to 6 servings

To Be as Cool as Can Be

1 onion
1 potato
2 beakers water
1 teaspoon salt
2 cucumbers
2 beakers milk
1 beaker sour cream
3 tablespoons chopped fresh dill
1 pinch pepper
1 dash **hardtoosaysaws**

Elementals

Kettle o' Cukes Soup*

*(That's wizard-speak for Chilled Cucumber-Dill Soup!)

1. Peel the onion and potato and cut into chunks. Put them in a medium-sized cauldron on the stove.

2. Add the water and salt and turn the burner to medium. Cook until potato pieces are soft. When done, set aside to cool.

3. Peel and cut the cucumbers into chunks. When the potato mixture is cool, puree in a blender with the cucumbers.

4. Stir in milk and sour cream, then add the dill and pepper.

5. Add the dash of ***hardtoosaysaws***. Pretend your wand is a fan and fan yourself with it while saying:

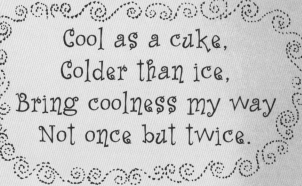

Cool as a cuke,
Colder than ice,
Bring coolness my way
Not once but twice.

6. Chill soup in refrigerator for a few hours before serving—until it is really cooooool!

Makes 6 servings

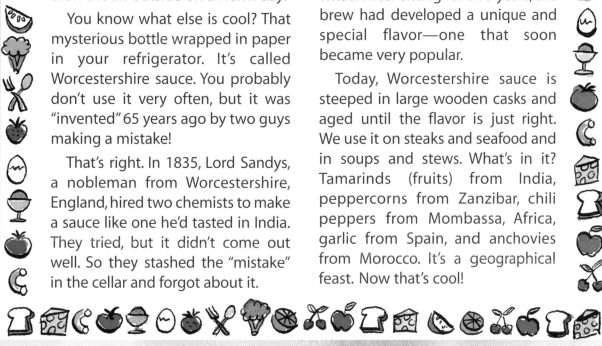

WAY COOL!

Ever hear the expression, "He's cool as a cucumber?" We say that because cucumbers really are cool inside—about 20 degrees cooler than the air outside on a warm day!

You know what else is cool? That mysterious bottle wrapped in paper in your refrigerator. It's called Worcestershire sauce. You probably don't use it very often, but it was "invented" 65 years ago by two guys making a mistake!

That's right. In 1835, Lord Sandys, a nobleman from Worcestershire, England, hired two chemists to make a sauce like one he'd tasted in India. They tried, but it didn't come out well. So they stashed the "mistake" in the cellar and forgot about it.

Two years later, one of them found the sauce again. Before throwing it out, he thought he'd have one more taste. And guess what? After sitting for two years, the brew had developed a unique and special flavor—one that soon became very popular.

Today, Worcestershire sauce is steeped in large wooden casks and aged until the flavor is just right. We use it on steaks and seafood and in soups and stews. What's in it? Tamarinds (fruits) from India, peppercorns from Zanzibar, chili peppers from Mombassa, Africa, garlic from Spain, and anchovies from Morocco. It's a geographical feast. Now that's cool!

To Keep Friends Forever

Dipped Cheese Sandwich

The wizard put two concoctions together for this recipe—
a grilled cheese sandwich and French toast. It makes a great
treat for lunch or a late-night sleepover.

2 eggs

1/3 beaker milk

1/2 teaspoon salt

8 slices cheese
(cheddar, American, or Swiss)

8 slices bread

1 smear *yelotangy*

2 tablespoons butter

Elementals

1. Crack the eggs on the edge of a shallow dish. Drop in the eggs and discard the shells. Beat the eggs briskly with a fork.

2. Stir in the milk and salt.

3. Put 2 slices of cheese between two slices of bread. Make four sandwiches this way.

4. Smear some *yelotangy* inside each sandwich.

Wave your wand with one hand and join your other hand with your friends as you say these magic words together:

New friends, old friends,
All together.
Let's stay good friends
Now and forever!

5. Heat a skillet on the stove top to medium heat.

6. Melt half of the butter (1 tablespoon) in the pan.

7. Using a spatula, dip a sandwich in the egg mixture so that it soaks briefly on both sides. (Be sure it stays together.) Put in pan, then do this for a second sandwich.

8. Grill the sandwiches in the skillet. When first side is golden brown, flip over and grill the other side, and remove to a plate.

9. Melt the rest of the butter in the pan, then soak and grill the other two sandwiches.

Makes 4 sandwiches

HOORAY FOR FAT?

Fat has gotten a bad "rap" lately. Everyone is trying to avoid eating it, and for good reason. Some kinds of fat are hard to digest. Eating too much can also clog your veins, so your blood doesn't run smoothly through your "pipes." And fatty foods can make you gain weight.

But fat isn't all bad! The fat that accumulates in our bodies helps cushion our bones and other organs. It protects us from feeling cold. And fat provides extra energy when we need it. That's because extra fat can be changed into body fuel. It doesn't give a quick burst of energy—like sugar gives. Fat takes longer to digest, so the food stays in your stomach longer—up to 4 or 5 hours! A meal with a lot of fat in it (like cheese and butter) keeps you feeling full for longer than a meal with less fat.

TRY THIS EXPERIMENT
Each time you get hungry between meals, have one of these snacks:
• a stalk of celery
• a slice or two of cheese
• a carrot
• a glass of milk

On a piece of paper, write what time you ate it and what time it was when you felt hungry again. Which foods kept you feeling full the longest?

25

To Make Imaginations Run Wild

1 head of lettuce
(whatever kind you like)

Add any or all of the following:

1 cucumber, peeled and sliced

1 tomato, sliced

1 yellow or red pepper,
seeded and sliced

1 red onion, peeled and sliced

1 scallion, sliced

1 bunch broccoli tops,
sliced into little florets

6 raw mushrooms, sliced

1 ripe avocado, peeled and cubed

a few artichoke hearts, cut in half

1/2 beaker cashew nuts

1/2 beaker smoked mozzarella
cheese, cut into cubes

1/2 beaker sprouts

2 hard-boiled eggs, sliced

1 can tuna fish, drained

1 beaker ham or turkey cubes

Elementals

Kitchen Sink Salad

1. Wash and tear your lettuce into medium-sized pieces.
2. Wash and prepare any of the other ingredients you want to toss in.
3. Create one of the great salad dressings below! That's where the magic comes in!

Before pouring your dressing potion over the salad, hold your wand over it and make a mixing motion in the air. Repeat these words:

Crisp, crunch,
lettuce munch,
Imaginations soar.
Tossed about
inside my head,
Create a mindful roar.

Serves 4 to 14 (depending on how many ingredients you put in!)

Vinaigrette *

2 tablespoons vinegar
1/2 teaspoon salt
1/2 beaker olive oil
1/2 teaspoon **mayksyasneez**

Mix the vinegar and salt in a small bowl and let stand for a few minutes. Add the oil and **mayksyasneez**. Stir hard with a fork or whisk, until the oil and vinegar mix.

Vinaigrette is a French word meaning "vinegar dressing."

Terrific Tahini

2 tablespoons olive oil
2 tablespoons tahini (sesame butter)
2 teaspoons soy sauce
2 tablespoons fresh **pukkerup**
1 clove garlic, minced
2 tablespoons water

Put all ingredients in a small bowl and stir together hard with a fork or whisk until well blended. Add more water as needed to get a good consistency for pouring.

OIL AND WATER DON'T MIX!

Did you ever hear the expression, "They're like oil and water"? It's usually said about two people who are very different from each other and don't get along. They "don't mix." Oil and water don't mix because the fat in oil doesn't dissolve well.

TRY THIS EXPERIMENT
Pour a spoonful of cooking oil into one beaker of cold water. What happens? The oil just sits there in a glob, floating on top of the water. If you try the same thing with hot water, the oil will break up a little bit into several smaller globs—but it still won't dissolve.

Now put a spoonful of vinegar into a clean beaker and add a spoonful of olive oil. Mix it with a fork. What happens? It breaks up quite a bit. So oil does mix with vinegar. That's because vinegar is an acid, and acids can break up oils. The same happens in your body. Acids in your stomach break up the fat into tiny globs, so you can digest it.

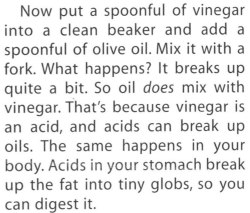

To Energize for Sports

Pa'sketti Marinara*
(*Translation: Spaghetti with Red Sauce!)

1 small onion

14.5-ounce can stewed tomatoes

2 tablespoons olive oil

6-ounce can tomato paste

1 beaker water

1 teaspoon dried oregano

2 cloves fresh garlic
(or 3/4 teaspoon garlic powder)

1/4 teaspoon salt

1/4 teaspoon pepper

2 teaspoons dried **bestoinpesto**

16-ounces spaghetti

grated cheese
(optional)

Elementals

1. Peel and chop onion; set aside.
2. If stewed tomatoes are not already chopped, cut into small pieces. (This is messy, so do it in a bowl.) Set the tomatoes aside.
3. Heat olive oil in large skillet over medium heat.
4. Add chopped onion. Stir and cook for 5 to 7 minutes, until onions are "see-through."
5. Add tomato paste, water, oregano, garlic, pepper, and stewed tomatoes.
6. Add **bestoinpesto** and stir.

Wave wand over your pa'sketti brew as if wafting the flavors toward your nose and repeat the following chant:

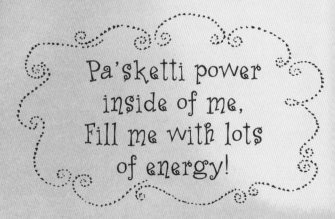

Pa'sketti power
inside of me,
Fill me with lots
of energy!

7. Lower heat to low, and cook (uncovered) for 20 minutes.

8. While sauce is simmering, fill a large cauldron 3/4 full of cold water, cover, and heat at high temperature on another burner.

9. When water boils, add spaghetti. Stir once to keep it from sticking to bottom.

10. Cook pasta 7 to 10 minutes (pot uncovered), or according to package directions.

11. Drain pasta in colander, rinse briefly with cold water, and shake to get extra water out. Transfer hot pasta to a serving bowl.

12. Serve spaghetti and sauce separately. It tastes better if sauce is put on at the last minute, not soaked through the spaghetti. Any extra sauce can be reheated for another meal.

13. Sprinkle grated cheese on top, if you like.

Makes 6 servings

SOME PRETTY OLD NOODLES?

Noodles are big all over the world, but the first dough for making pasta was probably invented in Italy in the 12th century. An old manuscript written in A.D. 1154 mentions the notorious noodle. In those days, flour was ground with stones and mixed with water; then the dough was cut into strips by hand and hung on trees to dry! When dried it could keep for months and years.

The best wheat for making pasta is a kind called *durum semolina*. All you really need for great noodles is flour and water, but some people add olive oil or an egg. Fancier pastas can be made with lemon and pepper, spinach, tomatoes, and even the black ink from squid!

Today, macaroni noodles come in nearly 100 different shapes—from geometric shapes of spirals and strands, to ribbons and rings, tubes and shells, wheels, letters, bow ties, and butterflies. Pasta is so popular that it has its own museum. In the city of Rome, you can visit the National Museum of Pasta Foods!

To Make Dreams Come True

Palm Reader's Pita Pockets

Sandwiches made with pitas are so much fun, because these flat breads from the Middle East have handy little pockets for stuffing. Start with cheese or chicken and e-x-p-a-n-d from there!

1. Cut off 1/2 inch along one side of the circular pita bread and open up the pocket.

2. Mix all ingredients together and stuff into the pita pocket.

3. When you add the special ingredient to each recipe, repeat these wishful magic words:

A pocket of magic,
A pita or two,
Help us to dream,
Make dreams come true.

Veggies with Cheese

1/2 beaker sprouts

1/2 beaker mixed raw veggies, chopped small (whatever you have: carrot, celery, broccoli, lettuce, zucchini, etc.)

1/2 beaker shredded cheese, any kind you like

2 tablespoons **noyamsiane**

Avocado Heaven

6 slices ripe avocado

3 slices Muenster cheese (or any other cheese you want

1/2 beaker sprouts

3 or 4 tomato slices

1 teaspoon **heltheeoyl**

Stuff these ingredients one at a time into pita.

Go Greek

1/2 beaker feta cheese
6 olives, chopped
1/4 cucumber, sliced
1 small tomato, sliced
2 tablespoons olive oil
1/4 teaspoon *rangooe*
1/4 teaspoon parsley
1 drizzle lemon juice

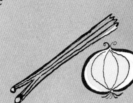

Chicken Salad

1 small breast cooked chicken, chopped or chunked
1 tablespoon mayonnaise
1/4 beaker chopped onion
1/4 beaker chopped celery
1 teaspoon chopped fresh *rymzwithfil*

GROW YOUR OWN

A sprout is made when a seed starts growing into a vegetable. Sprouts are easy and fun to grow—and they're loaded with good things to keep wizards healthy. Just buy some dry alfalfa seeds at your local health-food market and follow these steps to magically change the beans into sprouts!

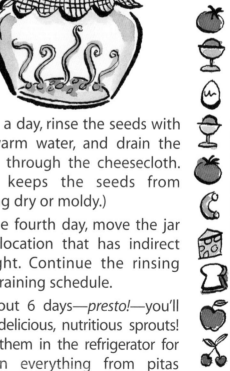

1. Rinse 1/4 beaker of dry seeds with water.

2. Put them in a bowl, covered with fresh water, to soak overnight.

3. The next day, use a strainer to drain off the water.

4. Put the damp seeds in a glass jar with cheesecloth covering the top of the jar. (Use an elastic band to keep the cheesecloth on.)

5. Put the jar in a dark, warm place (such as inside a kitchen cabinet).

6. Twice a day, rinse the seeds with lukewarm water, and drain the water through the cheesecloth. (This keeps the seeds from getting dry or moldy.)

7. On the fourth day, move the jar to a location that has indirect sunlight. Continue the rinsing and draining schedule.

8. In about 6 days—*presto!*—you'll have delicious, nutritious sprouts! Keep them in the refrigerator for use in everything from pitas to salads.

To Make a Surprise Arise

Taco Treasures

4 hard taco shells

1 beaker shredded cheese

1/2 beaker shredded lettuce

1/2 beaker tomato, chopped into small pieces

1/2 beaker chopped olives, green or black (optional)

1 avocado, peeled, pitted, and sliced (optional)

4 tablespoons *liddelbitthot*

Elementals

1. Warm your taco shells by placing them in a toaster oven on medium heat for 1 to 2 minutes.
2. When the taco shells are warm, move them to a plate.
3. Sprinkle 1/4 of the cheese, lettuce, and tomato across the center of the taco. If you wish to get more magical, add the olives and the avocado slices!
4. Spoon some *liddelbitthot* over top of each taco.

Wave wand back and forth over taco treasures and say:

Treasures and treats—
Bring me a surprise.
Cast something new
Before my eyes!

Makes 4

More Treasures!

If nonveggie tacos are more your style, sauté 3/4 pound of hamburger until well done and add some to each taco. You can keep adding more ingredients to your tacos until they're ready to burst the seams—cooked black or kidney beans, chili, chopped cucumbers, sour cream—you name it!

LETTUCE THINK ABOUT THIS

Ever notice what happens if you leave a lettuce leaf sitting out overnight on the counter? By morning it will be limp and not very appetizing. That's because lettuce is 90 percent water. Left out at room temperature, some of the water evaporates from the leaf, making it wilt.

To make a limp lettuce leaf crisp again, soak it in cool water. The leaf will absorb some of the water and get crisper and perkier with more water in it.

TRY THIS EXPERIMENT

1. Put one whole lettuce leaf on a plate.
2. Tear up another leaf and put the pieces on a plate too.
3. Let them stand for one hour at room temperature.
4. After the hour, which is crisper—the whole leaf or the pieces?

ANSWER: The whole leaf will be crisper. Why? Water escapes through the tears in a leaf. The more tears, the quicker it will wilt!

To see into the Future

Soothsayer's Spuds

4 large baking potatoes

3/4 beaker shredded cheese
(cheddar or mozzarella work best)

1/2 beaker milk

1 beaker cooked vegetables
(chopped broccoli or spinach)

1 pinch pepper

1/4 teaspoon
kristelshayks

Elementals

1. Preheat oven to 400 degrees.
2. Scrub potatoes, then prick them all over with a fork. (This helps them cook faster.)
3. Wrap each potato in tinfoil, place on oven rack, and cook for 1 hour. (To cook in microwave, DO NOT wrap in foil, just place potatoes in microwave and cook on high for 10 minutes or until tender.)
4. When done, let potatoes cool until you can handle them.
5. Cut cooled potatoes in half lengthwise. Scoop potato out of skins and place in a mixing bowl.

6. Mash potatoes. Add cheese, milk, cooked veggies, pepper, and stir.

7. Sprinkle mixture with **kristelshayks.**

Make sprinkling motion with wand and recite these magic words:

Show me the future,
Help me to see,
In years to come,
Where I might be.

8. Divide the mixture evenly among the potato halves and stuff them.

9. Place potatoes on a cookie sheet and bake 10 to 15 minutes more.

Makes 4 to 8 servings (depending on how stuffed you want to be!)

THE EYES HAVE IT

A soothsayer is a wise truth-teller who can often "see" into the future. In olden days (when wizards were everywhere), soothsayers were often blind. Their eyes could not see the world, but it was believed that they could see unseeable things more clearly than someone who was not blind.

Potatoes have eyes, but not the kind that can see. (Although, in some countries, people once thought spuds could tell the truth and predict the weather!) Potato eyes are really the buds of roots. If you want to grow more potatoes, plant ones that have sprouted lots of eyes.

Do you know where potatoes were originally grown? Ireland? Germany? Wrong! Potatoes were first grown in Peru, a country in South America. When potatoes were introduced to Europe, people didn't really like them. They thought they looked pretty funny—with their lumpy shapes and many eyes. Some people were terrified to grow them. The potato is in a family with another plant called "deadly nightshade." People feared the greens of the plant would poison them—until they discovered that the funny rounded roots were the tasty parts!

To Be the Best You Can Be

2 beakers cold water or chicken
broth (your choice)

1 tablespoon butter

1 beaker long-grain rice
(not instant or precooked)

1 pinch salt

half a 10-ounce package
frozen chopped spinach

4 scallions (green onions)

1/4 red or yellow bell pepper
(or both!), seeded

2 teaspoons chopped
leefeeyerb

Elementals

Glittering Rice

1. Put water or chicken broth and butter in medium cauldron. Heat to boiling.
2. Add rice and salt, stir. Return to boil.
3. Stir again and put a lid on cauldron.
4. Reduce heat to lowest temperature. Set timer for 20 minutes. Don't take lid off cooking rice (and definitely don't stir it!) until timer goes off.
5. Meanwhile, cook and drain spinach according to package directions.
6. Chop scallions and pepper(s) into very small pieces.
7. When timer goes off, stir in vegetable pieces and *leefeeyerb*.

Hold wand over Glittering Rice, touch your forehead with other hand, and repeat:

There's no harm in trying
To ace every test.
I'll aim for the sky,
And be the best!

8. Serve with Bubbling Sweet Beans.

Makes 4 servings

36

To Bubble Trouble Away

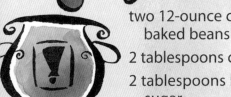

two 12-ounce cans baked beans

2 tablespoons catsup

2 tablespoons brown sugar

1/2 onion

2 tablespoons *murplesurple*

Bubbling Sweet Beans

1. Preheat oven to 350 degrees.
2. Open cans of beans, drain half the liquid off, and pour beans and remaining liquid into small ovenproof casserole dish.
3. Add catsup and brown sugar; stir.
4. Peel and chop onion into fine pieces; add to mixture.
5. Add *murplesurple* to the brew and stir.

Wave wand over bean brew, repeating these magic words:

Sweet beans bubble
My cares away.
Let nothing trouble
My mind today.

6. Bake for 30 minutes. Serve with Glittering Rice.

Makes 4 servings

PERFECT PROTEINS

Eating rice and beans in the same meal gives you a "perfect protein" combination. So what's a *protein*?

Protein is one of the "fuels" that keeps your body going. It is made up of building blocks called "amino acids," which form and repair human cells to keep us healthy.

Plants make their own protein from water, soil, and air. But people have to get protein by *eating* plants—or animals that have eaten plants. No plants have *all* the amino acids we need. But if you combine some in one meal—like rice and beans—you get a complete protein!

To Be an Amazing Cook

New Moon Noodles

1 stick butter

1 beaker heavy cream (or half-and-half)

1/4 teaspoon pepper

1 dash garlic powder

1 dash ground nutmeg

3/4 beaker **gudangreated**

16-ounce package fettuccini (the long, flat, wide noodles)

Elementals

1. Fill a large cauldron 3/4 full of cold water; cover and place on stove on high heat.

2. While water is heating, melt 1 stick of butter in smaller cauldron on medium-low heat.

3. When butter is melted, add heavy cream or half-and-half, pepper, garlic powder, and nutmeg. Stir.

4. Cook cream sauce for about 5 minutes, stirring often to keep it from burning. Do not boil.

5. Add **gudangreated** and stir the sauce some more.

As sauce starts to thicken, say the magic words. Wave wand above the pot and repeat three times:

Pastaspectaculo!
Give me the knack-ulo!

6. When water boils, add noodles. Stir once to keep noodles from sticking to bottom. Boil with the lid off, according to package directions.

7. Drain cooked noodles into a colander, then transfer to a serving bowl.

8. Add spectacular sauce and stir to coat every single noodle!

Makes 6 servings

TIPS FOR THE GOURMET WIZARD

Go ahead; get carried away! Here are some tips for master chefs.

Use fresh ingredients: Use fresh fruits and vegetables whenever you can. Foods that were just harvested have more vitamins and minerals than canned or frozen and are healthier.

Choose organic: Organic produce is grown without chemical pesticides, so it's better for you. If you can't buy organic, you might even start your own organic garden patch!

Have fun: Get a chef's hat and apron. Go to a cooking store and check out the gadgets! There are special tools for all kinds of cook's tasks. Save your allowance and treat yourself to some fun kitchen tools.

Get creative: Think of cooking as art class! Let your personal flair come out in your "presentation"—how food is arranged on the plate. Use garnishes, such as flowers and food decorations.

Get set: Make sure the table is set with everything you need before you sit down, so you won't have to jump up to get things. Try special dishes, a tablecloth, colorful napkins, and fresh flowers!

Don't go for perfection: It doesn't exist! Don't get discouraged if something you cook doesn't turn out "right" the first time. If you burn the food to a crisp, at least try to get a good laugh out of it. Then try again next time!

To Build Strong Muscles

Sorcerer's Spinach

1 bag fresh, washed spinach or 10-ounce box frozen, chopped

1/4 beaker soft cream cheese

1/4 teaspoon salt

2 tablespoons **notzozour**

1/4 beaker grated Parmesan cheese

1/4 beaker seasoned bread crumbs

1. Preheat oven to 350 degrees.
2. Put spinach in cauldron or skillet and add 1 to 2 inches of water.
3. Turn heat up to high and bring water to boil. Cook spinach until it is limp and soft.
4. Drain off the water by pouring the spinach into a colander. Shake it to get more drops of water out.
5. In a big bowl, combine warm, cooked spinach with soft cream cheese and salt.
6. Stir in **notzozour**.

Wave wand over the bowl with one hand, flexing your muscles, and recite the magical words at right.

Arms, legs, muscles, grow!
Make me strong
From head to toe!

7. Place spinach mixture in casserole dish and sprinkle Parmesan cheese and bread crumbs over the top.
8. Place casserole dish in oven, uncovered. Bake for 30 minutes, then enjoy!

Makes 4 side servings

To Sharpen Math Skills

6 ears corn
1/4 beaker ***maykzitsooeet***
6 tablespoons butter
salt and pepper

Conjurer's Corn

O KERNELS OF THOUGHT

If there are 650 kernels on the average ear of corn, about how many kernels would you have eaten if you polished off three whole ears of corn?

Figure It Out:

650 kernels
x 3 ears

Now how about if you split the next ear with someone. How many kernels would you each eat?

Figure It Out:

650 ÷ 2

So how many kernels did you chomp in all?

Figure It Out:

1,950
+ 325

ANSWERS: 1,950 kernels; 325 kernels; 2,275 kernels

1. Remove the husks and little silky threads from the corn. Rinse under water.
2. Place corn in a large cauldron and fill with enough water to cover it.
3. Heat water on high until it boils.
4. Pour in ***maykzitsooeet*** and stir. Wave your wand over the cauldron, repeating these words:

Abracadabra,
Abracazath,
Make me the best
In numbers and math!

5. Boil corn 5 to 10 minutes until corn is tender.
6. Carefully remove corn (use tongs—it's super hot!) and serve with butter, salt, and pepper.

Makes 6 side servings

To Ace Your Homework

1/4 pound shredded cheese (cheddar or Monterey Jack works best)

20 to 30 tortilla chips (nonflavored is best)

8-ounce can refried beans (optional)

1/2 beaker salsa (mild or hot—you choose)

handful of *laydeeuvpopiys*

Know-It-All Nachos

1. Preheat oven to 400 degrees.
2. Pour chips onto a pie plate or cookie sheet covered with foil (for faster cleanup).
3. If you're using refried beans, open can and scoop teaspoons of beans here and there over the pile of tortilla chips.
4. Drizzle salsa over everything and sprinkle shredded cheese over that.

Elementals

5. Slice **laydeeuvpopiys** and drop them around the dish.

With magic wand, make pretend check marks over the dish, saying:

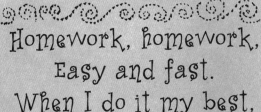

Homework, homework,
Easy and fast.
When I do it my best,
The knowledge will last.

6. Bake nachos for 5 minutes or so, just until cheese melts. (Check it often so it doesn't burn.)

7. When cool enough to touch, lift foil and move nachos to a plate to eat.

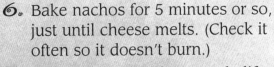

MYSTERY SPOT

Ever wonder what that spot is on a paper plate or towel when you finish the chips or fries? It's a grease mark, and it's one way to tell whether a snack or other food contains fat.

TRY THIS EXPERIMENT

1. Cut a brown paper bag into squares about 2 inches by 2 inches.

2. Rub any food you want to test against the brown paper. Here are some ideas:

   - tortilla chip
   - hunk of cheese
   - slice of raw potato
   - French fry
   - potato chip
   - piece of lettuce
   - pat of butter
   - slice of apple

3. Keep rubbing the piece of food until it leaves a wettish spot. If you're testing a lot of things, be sure to write what you're testing on each paper.

4. Let the papers dry overnight.

5. The next day, when you hold the paper up to the light, if you see a greasy spot on it, the food has fat in it!

43

To Share and Share Alike

toppings of your choice:
pepperoni or sausage
green pepper
olives
fresh tomato
mushrooms
cooked chicken (leftovers)
pineapple
onion
fresh garlic
fresh spinach leaves

2 English muffins

1/4 beaker pizza
or tomato sauce

1/4 beaker shredded
mozzarella cheese

2 pinches oregano

2 dashes powdered
smelyerb

Elementals

Pizza Pizzazz

1. Prepare all of the toppings you want to use (slice, dice, chop, chunk) and set them aside.
2. Preheat oven to "broil."
3. Cut English muffins into halves and toast in a toaster.
4. As soon as they pop up, spread pizza or tomato sauce on halves.
5. Sprinkle mozzarella cheese over the muffins.
6. Add toppings of your choice (mix it up!) and sprinkle a pinch of oregano on top of each one.

7. Sprinkle **smelyerb** over pizzas. Once they are totally pizzazzed, wave wand in pizza-sized circles over each one and repeat:

Share a little,
Share a lot.
Share together
What we've got!

8. Put pizzas on cookie sheet or pie tin and place under broiler for 1 to 2 minutes. Watch carefully—they can quickly burn!

Makes 4 little pizzas

PIZZA PIE CHARTS

There's nothing like a pizza pie for learning about fractions! Think of it this way:

When you buy a whole pizza, it's usually cut into 8 pieces, right? What part of the whole is each piece?

1 slice = 1/8

Suppose you eat two slices. What fraction of the whole pie is that?

2 slices = 1/4

You and a buddy together eat 4 slices. What part of the whole pizza is that?

4 slices = 1/2

Smelling the pizza, your big brother comes into the room and gobbles up 2 more pieces. How much of the pie is gone now?

6 slices = 3/4

Now the dog begs for a slice! If you give it to Fido, how much has been eaten now?

7 slices = 7/8

To Calm Your Worries

Wizard Wraps

2 soft tortillas (corn or flour)

choice of fillings:

peanut butter and apple

peanut butter and jelly or jam

peanut butter and bananas

peanut butter with honey ✗
and cinnamon *bananas*

peanut butter and celery

peanut butter and
marshmallow fluff

cream cheese and pineapple

cream cheese and smoked salmon

cream cheese and jelly or jam

cream cheese and
green olives *(try it!)*

cheddar cheese and avocado

cheddar cheese and sprouts

cheddar cheese and apple slices

mozzarella cheese and
pepperoni slices

generous helping of
wutweeawlnede

1. Lay your tortillas out.
2. Slice or chop any ingredients
   you've chosen to use.
3. Spread the peanut butter, cheeses,
   and other fillings on top.
4. Just before you roll them up,
   sprinkle liberally with
   wutweeawlnede.

Before digging in, wave your wand
in a flowing way and say:

Wrap my worries,
Send 'em away.
Make me feel calm
All through the day.

Homemade Peanut Butter

1 beaker unsalted,
shelled peanuts

1 tablespoon honey

3 tablespoons
vegetable oil

Put all ingredients into a blender and
mix on high for 1 minute. Stop the
blender now and then to pull peanuts
away from the sides. Refrigerate.

Elementals

FOOD ALLERGIES

A small number of people have a severe allergy to peanuts—and can even die from eating just half of one! That doesn't mean you have to be afraid of peanuts or peanut butter. For most people, they're very healthy foods. But it is good for you to know what an allergy is and who is allergic.

Being allergic to any kind of food means that if an affected person (about 1 in 10 children) eats certain foods, their bodies react by having a "symptom." Usually, the reaction occurs within minutes of eating the food they're allergic to.

Here are some symptoms to watch for:

• A tingling feeling in the lips or mouth after eating something

• An itchy rash or swelling that appears on your body

• Vomiting or nausea

• Stomach cramps or diarrhea

• Swelling in the throat, which makes it hard to breathe or swallow

The foods that most often cause allergic reactions include milk, eggs, wheat, things made from soybeans, fish, shellfish, peanuts, almonds, walnuts, and "MSG," a flavor helper.

Most kids "outgrow" food allergies by the time they are adults. That's because as we grow, our digestive systems "mature," and become better able to handle things that might have caused a problem when we were younger.

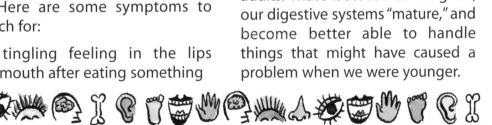

To Dare To Try Something New

Dungeon Dips

VEGGIES
carrot sticks
cucumber slices
celery sticks
broccoli florets
zucchini strips
raw mushrooms
snow peas
cauliflower florets
strips of red pepper
green beans

FRUITS
strawberries
apple slices
banana slices
pear slices
melon cubes
grapes
orange slices
cherry tomatoes

SNACKERS
tortilla chips
pita wedges
cubes of bread
potato chips
pretzels
crackers

1. Cut up your veggies or fruit into "dippable" pieces.
2. Make the dip of your choice, adding the magic ingredient last.

Before "dipping in," take magic wand in one hand and flit around the kitchen, saying:

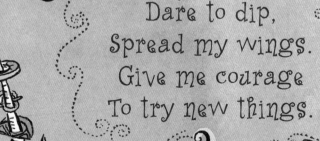

Dare to dip,
Spread my wings.
Give me courage
To try new things.

A VEGGIE OR A FRUIT?

Did you notice that we put tomatoes in the fruit category at left? If you thought they were vegetables, you're not alone. A lot of wizards (and nonwizards) get confused about this. We think of tomatoes as vegetables, because we eat them in veggie salads. Besides, tomatoes don't have a typical "fruity" sweet flavor. But actually, a tomato is a fruit of the tomato plant.

So what is the difference between a fruit and a vegetable? It might depend on whom you ask!

Definition 1 is general: Anything that doesn't have a sweet taste and that you eat in salad or as a side dish can be called a vegetable. Anything with sweet pulp eaten for dessert or as a snack is called a fruit.

Definition 2 is technical: A vegetable is part of a plant that is not able to reproduce on its own—such as a leaf, stem, root, or pod. A fruit is the part of a plant or tree that can reproduce more—the seed, the surrounding flesh, and any closely connected parts.

GUESS THIS

All righty, then: What is a pepper? A cucumber? A squash? An avocado?

If you guessed vegetable, you'd be generally right and technically wrong. If you guessed fruit, you'd be technically right and generally wrong. So you really can't win—or lose!

Guacamole Dip

Peel, pit, and mash avocados. Add everything else and stir well.

2 ripe avocados
(should be soft when you press on them)
1 clove garlic, minced
3 tablespoons fresh lemon juice
1/4 teaspoon pepper
1 pinch salt
2 tablespoons *leefeeyerb*

Humus Dip

Mash chickpeas and their liquid in a blender. Transfer to a bowl, then mix in rest of ingredients.

1 can chickpeas (with liquid)
1 beaker tahini (sesame butter)
2 tablespoons olive oil
juice from 2 lemons
2 garlic cloves, minced
salt to taste
1 tablespoon *curlyurby*

49

To Keep the Doctor Away

6 MacIntosh apples

1/4 beaker light brown sugar

1 1/2 beakers water

1/4 teaspoon *nomannic*

Elementals

Abracadabra Applesauce

1. Peel the apples. Cut them in half and cut out the core and seeds.
2. Cut apples into small pieces.

   Put apple pieces, light brown sugar, and water into a large cauldron on the stove.

3. Sprinkle in the **nomannic.** Wave your wand—with energy and a good healthy motion—over the apple mixture, declaring:

> Apple-ca-dabra
> Apple-ca-bray,
> Feeling good
> Every day.

4. Cook applesauce on medium heat for 15 to 20 minutes. (Keep checking; you may have to add more water so it doesn't burn.)

5. After apples are completely soft and mushy, mash them together and stir.

Makes 5 servings

HOW DO YOU LIKE THEM APPLES?

If you want to make enough applesauce to serve 50 people, using this recipe, how many apples would you have to buy?

How do you figure that out? First, divide 50 people by 5 people served by each batch of applesauce.

You get 10.

Second, multiply 10 batches of applesauce by 6 apples needed for each batch.

You get 60 apples.

Now try this: How many dozens of apples is 60 apples? Divide 60 by 12 (one dozen)

You get 5 dozen.

BONUS CHALLENGE

What if the apples were sold in bags of 9 apples each? How many bags of apples would you have to buy to make applesauce for 50 people? Divide 60 (number of apples needed for 50 people) by 9.

ANSWER: You get 6 bags plus 6 extra apples. So you'd have to buy 7 bags to get enough!

PLENTY OF LOVE POTIONS
To Bring Love into Your Life

These "love potions" will make you extra loving. Serve a potion to someone else, and they will love you for it!

1. Mix all the ingredients together in a blender and mix on high until frothy.
2. Just before serving, move your wand in heartfelt circles above the potion (secretly or out in the open) and repeat the love-ly words at right.

Love and kisses
Hugs and wishes—
Let them come to me!

Smoochers' Smoothie

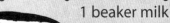

1 beaker milk

1 scoop vanilla ice cream

1/2 ripe banana

1 teaspoon *allinav*

Forbidden Forest Fizz

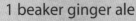

1 beaker ginger ale

1 beaker *sunnijoos*

2 ice cubes

You can make this one without a blender.

Peachy Keen Kisses

3 ripe peaches, peeled, with pits removed

1/3 beaker frozen pink lemonade concentrate

2 ice cubes

3/4 beaker *likwidaliyf*

Yummy Yogurt Shake

1 beaker strawberries, fresh or frozen and thawed

1 beaker pineapple juice

1 tablespoon honey

1/2 beaker plain *yoyogogo*

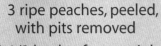

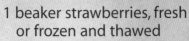

Elemental Egg Cream

The "egg cream" has neither eggs nor cream in it, so who knows how it got its name! It's basically a delicious ice cream soda without the ice cream.

- 1 beaker whole milk
- 2 tablespoons chocolate syrup
- 3/4 beaker *fizzeroo*

Stir the syrup into the milk (no blender), then add *fizzeroo* and watch it bubble!

Potion Pops

Here's a great way to magically change the form of any potion. Freeze it!

- 2 beakers any potion
- 4 paper cups
- 4 Popsicle sticks

Pour the mixture into paper cups. Put tinfoil over the top, make a slit in the center of the foil, and insert a stick through the slot. Freeze cups for 4 to 6 hours. Peel the foil off the cup and you're ready to slurp!

LOOK INTO MY CRYSTAL BALL

Wizards are sometimes called "shape-shifters" because they know how to make something change from one "shape" into another. Freezing liquid potions into frozen pops is one way to change forms. So is making crystal candy. Nonwizards would call this *crystallizing*.

TRY THIS EXPERIMENT

1. Put 1/2 beaker water in small cauldron on stovetop and heat on high till it boils.

2. Remove from heat and add 1 beaker sugar to the water.

3. Stir for 2 minutes to dissolve sugar.

4. When it is cool, pour sugar water into a clean quart-size glass jar.

5. Cut a 24-inch piece of cotton string and tie it to a chopstick. Lay the stick across the opening of the jar. Let the string hang down into the water and sugar mixture. (It can loop around in the bottom of the jar.)

6. Put the jar aside for 3 weeks or so. During this time, you can see crystals forming on the string.

7. When 3 weeks are up, remove the string and hang it so the crystals can dry.

Presto—crystal candy!

What happened? When you first stirred the sugar around in the water, it seemed to "disappear" as it dissolved. But it didn't really go away—it just became invisible. It got broken down into tiny particles that got absorbed into the water, or "dissolved." But once the water sat still awhile, those little sugar particles started "pulling together"—crystallizing—on the string!

Faerie Fruit Kabobs

8 strawberries, whole

8 chunks melon (cantaloupe and/or honeydew)

8 chunks other firm fruit, such as banana, peach, apple

12 **softanmushees**

4 long skewers

Chocolate Sauce (see below right)

1. Slip fruit on skewers, alternating types of fruit and **softanmushees**. Put each skewer on a serving plate.

Wave your magic wand up and down the side of each kabob and say:

> Kitchen kaboodle,
> Kabobbles of fun.
> We're ready to party
> Till the day is done.

2. Make the Chocolate Sauce and drizzle it while still warm over kabobs, turning them to coat all sides.

3. Let kabobs cool a bit before you slip each tidbit off onto your tongue!

Elementals

Chocolate Sauce

1 beaker chocolate chips

2 tablespoons buttermilk

Melt chocolate chips and milk together in small cauldron over low heat, stirring now and then with a wooden spoon.

Fruit Salad Silliness

What could refresh a wizard more than a cold, sweet fruit salad?

1. Take whatever fresh fruits you have in the house, peel and cut them into bite-sized pieces (except for the berries). Here are suggestions:

Apples	Bananas
Blueberries	Cantaloupe
Grapefruit	Grapes
Honeydew	Kiwis
Mango	Nectarines
Oranges	Peaches
Pears	Pineapple
Plums	Raspberries
Strawberries	Watermelon

2. Now add a few extras to jazz it up. Can't decide which ones to choose? Ask someone else to pick!

Chocolate chips	M & Ms
Maraschino cherries	Raisins
Mint leaves	Wheat germ
Shredded coconut	Walnuts
Mini-marshmallows	Almonds

3. Juice up your fruit salad with 1/4 beaker of honey, or orange juice mixed with a little brown sugar and cinnamon.

AWESOME OSMOSIS!

Did you ever notice that when you sprinkle sugar onto fruit salad, about 10 minutes later there is more juice? That's because of *osmosis!*

Osmosis is a natural process in which a weaker solution is drawn toward a stronger solution through a membrane with holes or openings in it. Osmosis happens a lot in plant and animal cells. The roots of a plant draw water from the soil by osmosis.

When you sprinkle sugar onto fruit, you create a stronger fruit-sugar solution on the outside of the fruit than what already exists inside. So some of the weaker fruit juice solution inside flows out through the tissue wall to join the stronger juice-and-sugar solution outside. There's really not more juice created, but because it's been pulled outside the fruit, you can see and taste it better!

To Make Something Creative

Mango-Tango Pudding

2 ripe mangos
2 tablespoons sugar
(optional)
1 beaker *ukanwippit*

Elementals

1. Peel the mangos, discard the seeds, and cut up the fruit.
2. Put the mango slices in a blender and blend until the fruit is mushy.
3. Taste. If it needs more sweetening, add the sugar.
4. Put *ukanwippit* into a bowl and whip with electric mixer until it "stands up" in peaks.
5. Stir mango mixture into the *ukanwippit*.

As you spoon the mango-tango into serving bowls, wave wand over this brilliant new concoction and, with great hope, declare:

Mango-tango, let me be
Filled with creativity
And endless possibility!

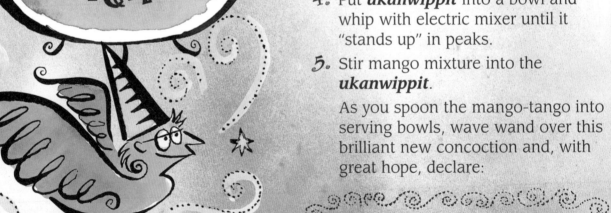

IT'S OOKEY-OOZE!

Mango-Tango Pudding is thickened with whipped cream. But some puddings use eggs or cornstarch to thicken them. Cornstarch can be so sticky, it's even put in glue. Eoow! Put it in cold water and it seems to dissolve. Heat it, and it expands. Is it a liquid or a solid—or something in between? Here's an ookey experiment that might help you decide:

- Put 2 tablespoons of room-temperature water into a small bowl.

- Add 5 tablespoons of cornstarch and mix well.

Over a bowl or sink, take the mucky cornstarch into your hand and roll it around fast. It will almost feel like it is a solid mass.

Stop moving the gunk around and what happens? It becomes kind of "liquid-y" and starts to ooze through your fingers, right? Pretty strange. So what is it—a solid or a liquid? (PS: Only the Most Masterful Wizard knows!)

To Clean Up in a FLASH

Bibbity-Bobbity Brownies

1 tablespoon vegetable shortening, or nonstick cooking-oil spray

4 squares of unsweetened baker's chocolate

1 stick butter

1 1/2 beakers sugar

2 eggs

2 tablespoons water

1 1/2 teaspoons vanilla extract

1 1/3 beakers flour

1/4 teaspoon baking soda

1/4 teaspoon salt

1/2 beaker chopped walnuts (optional)

1/2 beaker *chippitydippity*

Elementals

1. Preheat oven to 350 degrees.
2. Lightly grease a baking pan (8 inches square) by rubbing shortening all around on inside or spray with cooking-oil spray.
3. Put chocolate squares and butter into small cauldron and cook over low heat stirring to keep it from burning. When melted, set aside.
4. Put sugar, eggs, water, and vanilla into a separate bowl, and beat.
5. Stir the chocolate mixture into the sugar mixture.
6. Slowly add the flour, baking soda, and salt, stirring so they all blend.

7. Add nuts if you want them, and **chippitydippity**.

Move your wand like a feather duster over the batter, saying:

> Watch me scramble,
> Watch me scurry,
> Cleaning everything
> In a hurry!

8. Pour batter into greased pan; put in oven. Bake 25 to 30 minutes.

9. To see if it's done, stick a toothpick into the middle of the pan. If it comes out clean, the brownies are done. If it comes out with batter stuck to the sides of it, the brownies need a few more minutes in the oven.

Makes 12 brownies

Raspberry Swirls

To add something new and tasty to your brownies, try this: Before you put the batter in the oven, warm up 1/2 beaker of raspberry jam in a small cauldron on the stove. When it is warm and thinner, slowly pour it on the top of the pan in an S curve. Now pull a knife through the batter in an up-and-down pattern crosswise through the jam. When the brownies cook, they will have yummy swirls of raspberry all through them!

CHOCOLATE GROWS ON TREES?

In a way it does, but not in hanging chocolate bars! Chocolate is made from the seeds—the beans—of the cacao tree, which grows in warm parts of South America and Africa.

The native people in South America—the Mayans and Aztecs—grew cacao trees 1,400 years ago. They made a drink from the beans, called *xocolatl*. You can hear how the English word *chocolate* evolved from that word.

Sometimes *cocao* beans were exchanged like money. But the Aztecs believed that these seeds were sent from paradise and contained wisdom and power!

Around 1500, Christopher Columbus brought cacao beans and *xocolatl* back to Europe after visiting the New World, and chocolate drinks became popular. How did *cacao* become *cocoa*? Believe it or not, it was probably a spelling error made by the traders!

To See Things in a New Way

1 1/2 beakers sugar
3 tablespoons cocoa powder
4 tablespoons butter
1/2 beaker milk
1/2 teaspoon vanilla extract
1/2 beaker peanut butter
1/4 beaker raisins
3 1/2 beakers **otendoten**

Cosmic Cookies

These cookies are out of this world.
Not only because they taste so good,
but because they don't even need to
be baked!

1. Put sugar, cocoa, butter, and milk
   into a medium cauldron.
2. Bring to boil on stove top burner at
   medium-high heat.
3. Let it boil for only 1 minute, then
   remove from heat.
4. Add vanilla, peanut butter, raisins,
   and **otendoten**. Stir until peanut
   butter is melted, then let the batter
   cool just until it can be handled.

While the batter is cooling, wave
wand over the mixture and repeat:

Zing, zing, ala bingz,
It's all in how you look
at things!

Elementals

5. Form batter into balls and place on wax paper. Use spatula to flatten into cookies.

6. Chill in refrigerator for an hour before serving.

Makes 3 dozen

ARE YOU POSITIVE?

If you saw a glass of water filled halfway, would you say it was "half empty" or "half full?"

That may sound like just a twist of speech, but there's an important difference. If you see the glass as half empty, you're concentrating on its emptiness. If you see the glass as half full, you're concentrating on its fullness—and that's good!

A positive attitude has little to do with actual circumstances in your life. (The glass has the same amount of water in it either way.) Having a positive attitude is about how you look at things. Instead of seeing the "downside," look at the "upside."

For instance, if you're in the middle of making Cosmic Cookies and you realize you have no vanilla extract, you could see this as a big problem. "They're going to turn out all wrong! I'm a failure. I've let people down!" But with a positive attitude, you could say: "It'll be interesting to see how they turn out now! At least I'm trying. Maybe a friend can help me out; I'll see if someone else has vanilla. I'll still have something to contribute."

See the difference? Which way of reacting sounds like more fun? Which way is likely to have good results? Which one sounds more . . . cosmic?

To Make People LAUGH!

Snicker-Doodles

- 2 teaspoons shortening or nonstick cooking spray
- 1 stick butter
- 3/4 beaker sugar
- 1 egg
- 2 beakers flour
- 1 1/2 teaspoons baking powder
- 1/2 teaspoon salt
- 1/2 beaker milk
- 1/2 teaspoon vanilla extract
- 1 1/2 tablespoons sugar
- 1 teaspoon **nomannic**

Snicker-doodle was the funny name given to this cookie by Dutch settlers. Sometimes they called them an even funnier name—*kinkawoodles!* No wizard is really sure why, but it might be because the cookies wind up with silly-looking wrinkles on top after they have been baked.

1. Preheat oven to 325 degrees.
2. Grease two cookie sheets with the shortening or nonstick spray.
3. Cream butter and the 3/4 beaker sugar together with electric beaters until creamy and smooth.
4. Add egg and blend in quickly.
5. In a separate bowl, mix flour, baking powder, and salt.
6. In another bowl, mix milk and vanilla extract.

Elementals

7. Slowly mix the flour mixture into the butter/sugar mixture and blend well.

8. Now mix the milk mixture into it all and blend well.

9. Drop heaping teaspoonfuls of dough onto cookie sheet, about 2 inches apart.

10. Mix the 1 1/2 tablespoons sugar and **nomannic** and sprinkle over the top of the cookies.

   Hold your wand like a microphone and pretend to do a "stand-up comedy" routine. (It helps if you have an audience.)

Giggle and chuckle,
Snicker and scream.
Tee-hee, ha-ha,
To the extreme!

11. Bake cookies for 15 minutes. When golden brown on top, take out of oven (use mitts!) and remove from cookie sheet with a spatula to cool and wrinkle!

Makes 2 1/2 dozen cookies

BAKING POWDER POWER

Some breads are cooked with yeast, and the yeast makes the bread "rise," or puff up. Other breads and cakes are cooked with baking powder, which for a different reason also makes bread, cookies, and cakes "puff up."

How does baking powder work? It's made of two chemicals called *bicarbonate of soda* and *tartaric acid*. When those two get hot during cooking, they produce *carbon dioxide*—one of the gases in air. The air bubbles make the cookies "rise"!

When you cook pancakes with baking powder in them, you can actually see the bubbles of air forming as the batter heats up. Bubbles form in the cookies too; you just can't see them because the oven door is shut!

Smooshy S'mores

8 graham cracker squares (4 whole crackers broken in halves)

foil squares (each about 8 inches square)
(*Wax paper squares if you're using microwave method*)

4 squares dark or milk chocolate, each about 3" x 3"

2 marshmallows, cut in half so you have 4 flatter marshmallows

handful of *tineedryds*

Elementals

1. Preheat toaster oven (or regular oven) to 300 degrees.
2. Put each graham cracker on a piece of foil.
3. Place chocolate square on the graham cracker.
4. Place half a marshmallow on top of the chocolate.
5. Place a few *tineedryds* on the graham cracker too.

Wave wand in circles around your tummy and say:

> In the dark
> Or by firelight,
> With s'mores I'm fearless
> All through the night!

6. Put another graham cracker on top of each prepared one.
7. Fold the foil around each s'more and bake 5 minutes till chocolate melts.
8. Remove foil and enjoy (be careful; it's hot).

MICROWAVE METHOD

1. Prepare the same as on page 64, except build the s'more on a square of wax paper, not on foil. When "cookie" is complete, fold the wax paper around the s'more to catch any drips.

2. Put wrapped s'more on a microwaveable plate.

3. Microwave for 45 seconds, until chocolate is melted.

Serves 2 or 4 (You can always make s'more!)

S'WHAT ARE S'MORES?

You know what's in 'em, but do you know the history? Marshmallows have been around since the 1880s. So s'mores could be at least that old. The first published recipe for these cookielike treats appeared in the 1940 edition of the Girl Scout Handbook. And people have been slurping them down around campfires ever since.

Chocolate goes way back, but what about graham crackers? These tasty crackers are made from graham flour, a coarsely milled whole wheat flour that has more "bran" (the skin or husk of the grain) left in than other flours.

A 19th century doctor named Reverend Sylvester Graham urged people to eat graham products, as part of his campaign against white flour. "Thousands of people," he wrote, "eat the most miserable trash that can be imagined, in the form of bread, and never seem to think that they can possibly have anything better, nor even that it is an evil to eat such vile stuff as they do!"

Modern-day graham crackers now are so refined, however, they have lost much of their benefits. What would Reverend Graham say about that?

To Bring On Beautiful Weather

1 teaspoon butter
6 to 8 MacIntosh apples
1 beaker flour
1 beaker sugar
1 teaspoon baking powder
1/4 teaspoon cinnamon
1/4 teaspoon *megnut*
1 egg
1/2 stick butter

Elementals

Apple Cauldron Cobbler

1. Preheat oven to 375 degrees.
2. Butter a baking dish.
3. Peel the apples and remove the cores and seeds. Chop apples into bite-sized pieces.
4. Spread the apples around the bottom of the baking pan.
5. In a bowl, mix together the flour, sugar, baking powder, and cinnamon
6. Sprinkle in the **megnut**.

Wave your wand in "crisp" strokes back and forth and say with sureness:

Wind and clouds
And storms away!
Bring the sun
To shine my way!

7. In another bowl, beat the egg, then add it to the flour mixture and blend it in.

8. Drop the batter in little clumps on top of the apples.

9. Cut the butter into little chunks and "dot" the top of the batter.

10. Put dish in oven and bake 20 to 25 minutes.

Makes 6 cobbler servings

TEMPERATURE SCALES

When you want to "bring on beautiful weather" you might think of a crisp, shining day in apple season. The temperature then is usually around 75 degrees Fahrenheit.

We say "Fahrenheit" after a temperature because there is more than one measuring scale. The Fahrenheit scale was introduced in 1714 by a man named (you guessed it!) Fahrenheit. Daniel Gabriel Fahrenheit was a German-born scientist who lived in Holland. The coldest temperature he could create in his lab with a mixture of ice and salt is what he called "0" degrees. The U.S. uses the Fahrenheit system.

The Celsius scale was developed by a man with the name of (yup!) Celsius. Anders Celsius was a Swedish astronomer who introduced his scale in 1742. He used the temperature at which water freezes as "0" on his scale, and the temperature at which water boils as "100." (This scale is also sometimes called *centigrade*.) The Celsius scale is part of the "metric system" of measurement and is used in most of the world—but not in the United States.

100° / 212°

0° / 32°

To Convert Fahrenheit to Celsius :

- Subtract 32 from the Fahrenheit temperature.
- Multiply that sum by 5.
- Divide that sum by 9.

To Convert Celsius To Fahrenheit:

- Multiply the Celsius temperature by 9.
- Divide that sum by 5.
- Add 32.

MATH CHALLENGE

If it's 35 degrees Celsius, should I plan a ski trip?

ANSWER: No. Plan a trip to the beach; it's 95 degrees F!

To Make You Jump for Joy

shortening or nonstick
cooking spray

4 eggs

3/4 beaker sugar

1 teaspoon vanilla

3/4 beaker flour

3/4 teaspoon baking powder

1/2 teaspoon salt

1/4 beaker **kunfekshunario,**
in a shaker or sifter

1/2 beaker jelly or jam

Elementals

1. Preheat oven to 375 degrees.
2. Line a baking sheet (10 x 15 inches) with foil, extending it over the edges of the baking sheet.
3. Grease the foil with shortening or cooking spray.
4. Separate the egg yolks from the egg whites in two different bowls. (Have a grown-up wizard show you how to do this—it's tricky!)
5. Beat the yolks, add the sugar, and beat again until creamy.
6. Add vanilla and stir in well.
7. In a separate bowl, mix together the flour, baking powder, and salt.
8. Add flour mixture gradually to the egg mixture. Beat until smooth.
9. With electric mixer, whip the egg whites till they make stiff peaks.
10. "Fold" the egg whites into the cake batter by turning the white clouds in slowly.
11. Pour batter onto the greased, foil-covered baking sheet. Put pan into the oven and bake 12 minutes or until a toothpick inserted comes out clean.

12. As soon as you take cake from oven, loosen the edges from the foil with a spatula and dust the cake with **kunfekshunario**.

Wave wand over cake, and jump up and down while singing out:

> Jelly roll jump,
> Jelly roll jazz,
> Fill me with joy
> And razz-a-ma-tazz!

13. Spread jelly or jam over the cake, being careful not to tear it.

14. Holding the short edge of the foil, roll the cake up while it's still warm. Slice into 10 pieces.

Makes 10 joyful jelly rolls

GO FIGURE!

How many square inches of cake are you rolling up to make jelly rolls? We figure square inches by multiplying the length of a rectangle or square by its width.

For example, if the cookie sheet you're using is 10 inches by 15 inches:

Multiply 10 x 15

You get: 150 square inches of cake overall.

Math Tip: Whenever you want to multiply a number by 10, simply add a "0" to the original number. So to multiply 15 by 10, take the 15 and add a 0. How easy is that?

BONUS CHALLENGE

How many square inches of cake are in each piece of the jelly roll?

Divide 150 square inches by the number of rolls (10).

You get: 15 square inches in each piece.

Math Tip: To divide by ten, just take away the 0. Just as easy, isn't it?

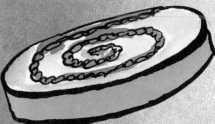

BEDTIME BREWS
To Bring On a Good Night's Sleep

Nodding Nightcap

1 beaker water

1 tea bag camomile* tea

1/2 teaspoon **bizybeezmaykit**

Camomile is a very mild herb that helps people relax.

1. Put water in a small cauldron or teapot and bring to a boil.
2. Put tea bag in mug, then add boiling water.
3. Let tea "brew" for about 3 minutes.
4. Remove tea bag.
5. Add **bizybeezmaykit** and stir.

With heavy eyes half closed, wave your wand in the steam of the tea and say:

Pillow soft and cozy bed,
Make we want to rest my head.
Whisper softly, not a sound,
Let the mists of sleep surround!

Makes 1 serving

To Bring On Magical Dreams

Dreamtime Dregs

2 beakers apple cider
2 whole cloves
1/2 cinnamon stick
1 dash nutmeg
2 teaspoons fresh *pukkerup*
2 slices lemon (optional)

1. Put cider, cloves, cinnamon, and nutmeg in a small cauldron.
2. Add fresh *pukkerup.*
   Wave your wand and say:

> Sim, sim, ala bim,
> Close my eyes when lights go dim.
> Beem, beem, ala zeem,
> Bring to me a magic dream!

3. Heat on medium-low for 10 minutes. Do not boil.
4. Strain cider and pour into mugs.
5. Slit each lemon slice and place one over the lip of each mug.

Makes 2 spicy cups

GO WITH THE FLOW

Thick liquids, such as honey, have *viscosity*. What does that mean? Viscosity has to do with how quickly or slowly a liquid flows or something moves through it. If it flows slowly, we say it is "viscous."

TRY THIS EXPERIMENT

1. Get 3 clean juice glasses and 3 small marbles.
2. Fill one glass with water, one with honey, and one with maple syrup.
3. Drop a marble into each glass at the same time. Watch how quickly or slowly the marble travels through the liquid.

QUESTION

Which liquid—water, honey, or maple syrup—was the *most* viscous? In other words, which one made the marble move most slowly?

Which liquid was the *least* viscous?

ANSWERS: the honey; the water

To Make World Peace

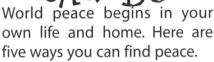

Peace Potion

2 beakers milk

2 heaping tablespoons sugar

2 heaping tablespoons *chakalada*

2 dashes cinnamon

1/4 teaspoon vanilla extract

whipped cream (optional)

1. Put milk into small cauldron on medium heat.
2. Heat, stirring often, but do not boil.
3. Put half of the sugar and half of the *chakalada* into one mug and half into another.

With your wand, make a peace sign in the air and recite:

> You do your part,
> I'll do mine.
> We'll build world peace,
> One piece at a time!
> Harmoniamundia!

4. Add a little hot milk, stir to blend, then add the rest of the milk.
5. Add half of the cinnamon and vanilla to each cup. Stir, and top with whipped cream!

WHAT YOU CAN DO

World peace begins in your own life and home. Here are five ways you can find peace.

1. *Be willing to listen.* Try this powerful peace tool: Just listen and don't react. Listening doesn't mean you have to agree.

2. *Practice doing nice things—without being asked.* Hold a door, shovel a sidewalk, or make a call. It feels good, so it's nice for you too!

3. *Focus on the positive in others.* Instead of noticing what you don't like, see the positive! Try to "catch" someone doing something you can compliment. Say it out loud, and peace will increase!

4. *Develop "wizard power" within.* True power is not power over people but the power within to be your best self! So pay attention to your own life and actions.

5. *Breathe deeply.* When people are upset, they often breathe shallowly. This can make you agitated and more likely to hurt others. Next time you're upset, remember to breathe!